# REBUILDING UNDER DEBT

## THINKING CLEARLY WHEN EVERYTHING IS A BLUR

CECILIA REGINA AQUINO BLANQUERA

**Disclaimer**

*This book is for informational and educational purposes only. It does not constitute financial, legal, or professional advice. The author and publisher disclaim any liability arising directly or indirectly from the use or application of this material.*



*Blanquera, Cecilia Regina Aquino*

*Rebuilding under debt : thinking clearly when everything is a blur / Cecilia Regina Aquino Blanquera. -- Calamba City, Laguna : Cecilia Regina Aquino Blanquera, [2026], ©2026. pages ; cm*

*ISBN 978-621-06-5067-9 (epub)*
*ISBN 978-621-06-5068-6 (softbound/paperback)*
*ISBN 978-621-06-5069-3 (pdf/downloadable)*

*1. Debt 2.Debt relief 3.Decision making 4.Finance, Personal.*

*I. Title.*

*332.02402 HG3755.3 2026 P320260025*

*First edition: 2026*

*Published by: Cecilia Regina Aquino Blanquera*

*Calamba City, Philippines*

*hello@steadyhandpress.com*

*Join the newsletter for updates, resources and new releases:*

*join.steadyhandpress.com*

*For Emilio*

*May you never have to read this*

SCAN to JOIN
the newsletter for updates, resources
and new releases:

join.steadyhandpress.com

A *BLUR* BOOK

# A BLUR BOOK

*BLUR BOOKS were written for moments when clarity collapses. When pressure outpaces perspective, timelines compress, and the cost of being wrong feels heavier than usual. In those conditions, thinking degrades—not because you're incapable, but because the environment itself is hostile to good judgment.*

*Throughout history, humans have made their worst decisions not in ignorance, but under strain. The Blur is what happens when urgency crowds out orientation. This book exists to slow that moment down—to restore enough clarity that you can choose your next step without making things worse.*

# REBUILDING UNDER DEBT

## THINKING CLEARLY WHEN EVERYTHING IS A BLUR

**Cecilia Regina Aquino Blanquera**

# ABOUT THE BOOK

**Rebuilding Under Debt** is not a success story.

It doesn't promise a way out in ten steps. It doesn't assume clarity, confidence, or momentum. And it doesn't pretend that financial crisis is only a math problem waiting to be solved.

This book is written for moments when pressure is high, clarity is low, and most advice feels unusable.

Debt—especially prolonged debt—creates a specific kind of cognitive environment. Decisions carry heavier consequences. Small mistakes are expensive. Urgency crowds out judgment. In these conditions, the usual language of motivation, hustle, and optimization often makes things worse.

This book starts from a different premise:

When the situation cannot yet be solved, **the priority is to avoid making it worse**.

Rather than focusing immediately on outcomes, **Rebuilding Under Debt** introduces the idea of *positioning*—how to stand, decide, and act when conditions are unstable. It distinguishes between motion and progress, between action that reduces harm and action that simply relieves anxiety. It names drifting as a greater long-term danger than failure, and it treats restraint as a legitimate form of responsibility.

The frameworks in this book are not designed for ideal circumstances. They are designed to survive bad days.

You'll find:

- ways to reduce exposure before chasing solutions
- tools for preserving judgment under pressure
- guidance for evaluating opportunities when urgency distorts perception
- systems that hold up even when energy, motivation, or confidence fluctuate

Personal experiences may appear in this book, but only as anchors—not as the point. The goal is not to persuade through story, but to translate lived pressure into structures that others can adapt to their own situations.

This is not a book about winning.

It's a book about staying intact long enough for better decisions to become possible.

If you're looking for inspiration, there are many books that do that well. If you're looking for certainty, this book won't offer it. But if you're in a season where everything feels blurred—financially, emotionally, or cognitively—this book is meant to give you something steadier than hope: orientation.

Not a way out but a way to stand.

# AUTHOR'S NOTE

This book was written during rebuilding, not after it — under real financial pressure, not from a place of resolution.

From inside the process, decisions still carried weight, margins were thin, mistakes cost more, and certainty was in short supply. What this book offers is not a success story, but a record — a testament to the quiet strength that comes from positioning yourself steadily within the storm.

If calmer waters now lie ahead, it's because rebuilding did its job. Growth can begin later — but only if one can survive long enough for it to become possible.

This book isn't about the victory lap in the end. It's also not about the urge to "throw the towel" early on. It's about what one can do during the long pause in the middle that nobody likes to talk about.

It's about surviving intelligently to rebuild with dignity while waiting for the coast to clear.

Everything here comes from lived constraint, not theoretical distance. The frameworks in this book were shaped while tradeoffs were real and outcomes were still unresolved. If parts of it feel cautious or unglamorous, that's because caution is often the most ethical response to risk — especially when the cost of being wrong is high.

This book does not promise transformation. It offers orientation. Its aim is not to push you forward, but to help you stop making things worse — and then, quietly and carefully, make them better.

If this book helps you slow down at the right moments, avoid unnecessary damage, or trust your own judgment a little more under pressure, then it has done its job.

# CONTENTS

# INTRODUCTION

**How to Use This Book**

This book is not meant to be read quickly. It is designed to function as a guide.

It's meant to be **returned to.**

You don't need to agree with everything in it all at once. You don't need to apply every framework immediately. In fact, trying to "do it properly" from the start often defeats the purpose.

It exists to help you think more clearly when **pressure is high and margin is low**. That means it will be most useful at moments when you feel stuck, rushed, overwhelmed, or uncertain — not when everything feels calm.

Some people will read it straight through. Others will open it only when something feels off and read a single chapter. Both approaches are valid.

What matters is not completion.

What matters is **orientation.**

You'll notice that many sections are written to slow you

down rather than push you forward. That's intentional. Under debt and constraint, speed is rarely the missing ingredient — **accuracy is**.

If you find yourself returning to the same chapter more than once, that's not a failure of progress. It's a sign that you're using it correctly.

This is not a book about getting ahead.

It's a book about **not making things worse** — and then, quietly and carefully, making them better.

## Getting the Most Out of This Book

- Read with a pen nearby (or use the highlight feature if you're reading this on an e-reader). Not to underline everything, but to note where you feel resistance or relief. Those reactions are information.

- Use the frameworks selectively. You don't need all of them at once. One good filter, applied consistently, is more powerful than ten applied sporadically.

- Revisit chapters as circumstances change. A chapter that didn't resonate early on may become essential later.

- Don't rush to act. This book is designed to improve judgment first. Action comes later — and more safely.

Above all, treat this book as a guide and a **companion**, not a checklist.

It's here to help you make decisions you won't regret — even on days when clarity is hard to come by.

# HIGH-CONCEPT SKILLS FOR LIFE UNDER CONSTRAINT

## The Skills This Book Builds

When life is tight, advice often turns blunt: cut everything, hustle harder, push through.

The problem is that constraint doesn't just limit money — it also limits attention, energy, emotional bandwidth, and margin for error.

That's why survival is not only a financial task. It's a design task. A thinking task. A "meaning" task.

The goal here isn't to become "more productive." It's to become more durable.

Below are **six skills** that quietly matter more when resources are limited — because they help you rebuild without breaking yourself. This book aims to help you develop these skills quietly and confidently, page by page.

## High-Concept Skills for Life Under Constraint

### 1) Design

**Build systems that can survive a bad month.**

In constraint, "design" means shaping your life so it still holds under pressure. You're not trying to create the perfect plan. You're creating a structure that doesn't collapse when something goes wrong.

Design looks like:

•*budgets that don't require heroics to maintain*

•*routines that protect energy and attention*

•*plans with slack, backups, and exit ramps*

•*a "minimum viable stability" setup you can keep even on low-capacity days*

The question is always: What can I maintain when I'm tired, stressed, and not at my best?

### 2) Story

**Reframe your story without self-deception.**

Story is not about sugarcoating. Story is the narrative you live inside — the one that determines whether you act with agency or shame.

A stable story under constraint:

•*removes moral drama from hard choices*

•*avoids pretending everything is fine*

•*names uncertainty without collapsing into panic*

•*keeps your identity separate from your current numbers*

The point is to tell the truth in a way that doesn't destroy your will to continue.

### 3) Symphony

**See the system, not just one problem.**

Constraint creates tunnel vision. Symphony is the ability to zoom out and see how the parts interact.

This matters because money is rarely "just money." It's tied to:

•*sleep and cognitive clarity*

•*family obligations and emotional labor*

•*self-respect, fear, and avoidance*

•*habits that either stabilize or destabilize you*

Your job is not to optimize one metric. It's to coordinate the whole system so it stops bleeding.

### 4) Empathy

**Treat caution as an ethical response.**

Empathy here includes self-empathy — not indulgence, but respect for limits.

Empathy means:

•*you don't punish yourself into compliance*

•*you don't treat burnout as a motivational failure*

•*you stop using shame as fuel*

•*you build rules that protect you from your own panic*

Constraint requires realism. Realism requires kindness that doesn't lie.

### 5) Play

**Use micro-experiments, not grand reinventions**

When stakes are high, people swing between paralysis and overcorrection. Play breaks that cycle by making change small, reversible, and informative.

Play looks like:

•*testing one income lever for 2 weeks*

•*negotiating one bill*

•*trying one boundary*

•*changing one habit and observing the effect*

You're not gambling your future on a single dramatic move. You're collecting data with low risk.

## 6) Meaning

**Anchor your actions in dignity, not outcomes.**

Meaning is what keeps you from trading your future self for short-term relief.

Under constraint, meaning is:

•*refusing choices that require self-betrayal*

•*protecting dignity even when you can't be "impressive"*

•*prioritizing stability because it keeps you alive long enough for growth to become real*

The goal isn't to win. It's to rebuild without losing yourself.

These six skills help you think clearly while visibility is low, preserve agency under pressure, and build a personal truth-filter that can survive hard seasons.

Constraint is not the end of your life.

But it is a test of whether your systems — and your self-respect — can hold.

# THE THREE CORE CONCEPTS

## I. THE BLUR

### The Hostile Environment

When you're under debt, the hardest part is not the numbers.

It's that everything starts to blur together.

Decisions that used to feel manageable now feel loaded. Small choices carry outsized consequences. Your mind runs background calculations you didn't consent to—bills, timelines, risks, what happens if this fails, what happens if it works but not fast enough.

. . .

In that state, most advice makes things worse. It tells you to be confident, to push harder, to move faster—exactly when your judgment is under the most strain.

The Blur is what happens when pressure outpaces clarity. When timelines compress, consequences grow heavier, and your mind is forced to carry too many variables at once. It isn't confusion, and it isn't failure. It's what happens to any human system when margin disappears.

The Blur is having a tight chest as soon as you wake up in the morning. It's the sheer terror you feel at the sound of a ringing phone. Some days it's a feeling of hectic panic. Most days, it's the feeling of helpless surrender as you stare blankly into space, so surreal that you disassociate from reality in a split second.

The danger of The Blur isn't that you can't act—it's that you act too quickly, without the perspective your situation actually requires. This book exists to slow that moment down, long enough for judgment to return.

This book is not here to motivate you. It's here to help you think clearly again, when clarity feels least available and mistakes are no longer cheap.

## II. POSITIONING

### What To Do When the Problem Can't Be Solved Yet

. . .

When pressure rises, the instinct is to fix. To act. To move. To solve something—anything—so the sense of helplessness eases. But there are moments when the problem cannot yet be solved, only survived. In those moments, action taken too early doesn't create progress. It increases exposure.

This chapter is about what to do when clarity hasn't returned, solutions are unreliable, and even good intentions carry risk. It's about positioning—choosing where to stand while conditions remain unstable, so you don't make the situation worse while waiting for it to change.

## Purpose of the chapter

To give you:

- permission to stop fixing prematurely
- a way to act *without escalating risk*
- a stable stance before introducing any frameworks

## *A. The reflex to fix—and why it fails under pressure*

- Humans equate motion with safety
- Debt and crisis compress time perception
- "Doing something" becomes emotional regulation, not strategy

Under constraint, urgency often feels like responsibility—but it isn't.

### *B. What positioning actually is*

- Positioning is not avoidance
- Positioning is not waiting for permission
- Positioning is not passivity

**Positioning is choosing where to stand when the situation itself is unstable.**

Consider this seamanship analogy:

- A sailor doesn't solve the storm
- They manage exposure, angle, and survivability
- The goal is staying upright, not arriving faster

### *C. What good positioning looks like*

- narrower exposure
- preserved optionality
- protected judgment
- energy conservation without collapse

### *D. Why positioning comes before every other chapter*

- The rest of the book assumes positioning is in place
- Frameworks fail when applied from panic
- Positioning makes later tools usable

You don't position yourself to avoid action. You position yourself so action doesn't cost more than it's worth.

When the storm is active, your responsibility isn't to win. It's to remain intact enough to make good decisions later. Positioning is how you do that. It keeps you from drifting, from escalating harm, and from mistaking motion for progress. Everything that follows in this book assumes you've done this first—because without positioning, even good advice can make things worse.

## III. DRIFTING

### Why Failure Isn't the Real Danger

Purpose of this chapter

- To remove the fear of "doing nothing"
- To redefine danger under pressure

- To explain why motion can be more harmful than mistakes

Most people aren't undone by failure. Failure is visible. It has edges. You can name it, assess it, and learn from it. What causes real damage during prolonged pressure is something quieter and harder to detect: **drifting**.

**Drifting** is what happens when action continues but orientation is lost. When urgency makes decisions for you. When movement replaces direction. You're not frozen—you're busy—but nothing is stabilizing.

### *A. Why failure gets blamed (and drifting doesn't)*

- Failure is concrete; drifting is ambient
- Failure feels dramatic; drifting feels normal
- Failure invites reflection; drifting erodes it

Failure often stops you. Drifting keeps you going in the wrong direction.

### *B. What drifting actually looks like (very important)*

Examples:

- taking on side projects "just in case"
- saying yes to opportunities you don't have capacity for
- making financial moves to relieve anxiety, not risk
- constantly researching instead of orienting
- staying busy to avoid sitting with uncertainty

Drifting feels productive because it creates motion. It feels responsible because it responds to pressure. But it quietly increases exposure.

### *C. Why drifting feels safer than stopping*

- stillness evokes fear of imminent unknowns
- movement gives the illusion of control
- society rewards visible effort, not quiet restraint

Drifting is not a character flaw. It's a stress response.

### *D. The cost of drifting (what it erodes)*

Drifting erodes:

- judgment

- energy
- optionality
- trust in your own decisions
- the ability to recognize good opportunities later

Drifting doesn't usually cause collapse. It prevents recovery.

### *E. The alternative to drifting (without heroics)*

- stopping to orient is an action
- refusing to escalate is a decision
- containment is not surrender

Positioning interrupts drift without demanding certainty.

Under pressure, your task isn't to avoid failure at all costs. It's to avoid losing orientation. Failure can be absorbed. Drift compounds. Positioning is what keeps you reachable by future clarity—so when conditions change, you're still in a place where better decisions are possible.

### *F. Positioning vs drifting (critical distinction)*

- Pausing ≠ drifting

- Choosing not to act ≠ surrender
- Orientation ≠ indecision

**Drifting is movement without orientation.**
Examples of drifting:

- saying yes to relieve anxiety
- chasing options just to feel momentum
- letting urgency choose for you

Most people aren't undone by a single bad decision either, but by a series of un-positioned reactions.

## WHEN EVERYTHING IS A BLUR

### A NO-NONSENSE DECISION CHECK FOR HIGH-PRESSURE MOMENTS

Some readers find it helpful to have a simple reference during high-pressure moments—something they can return to when thinking feels fragmented. The mini-guide that follows shows the relationship between The Blur, positioning, and drifting. It distills the core idea of positioning into a single check. It's not meant to replace the chapters that follow, only to anchor them.

**1. Pressure exceeds clarity.**
You are not failing. The environment is unstable.

**2. Pause before solving.**
A choice exists before action.

1. **Ask:** *Am I acting to reduce urgency—or to reduce harm?*

2. **If acting prioritizes reducing urgency →** **PAUSE**. You're on **DRIFTING** territory where:

- Exposure increases
- Judgment erodes
- Options shrink

3. **If acting prioritizes reducing harm → PROCEED. You're in POSITIONING mode in which:**

- Exposure narrows
- Judgment is protected
- Options remain

**RULE:** Do not make the situation worse while waiting for clarity. Always ensure you're prioritizing "decision safety" over impulsive actions driven solely by fear or urgency.

# THE REBUILDING TRIAGE

## A PRACTICAL FRAMEWORK FOR WHEN YOU CAN'T AFFORD ANOTHER FAILURE

**PHASE 1: THE ACCURACY CHECK** (Stop the Bleeding)

When you feel the urge to act immediately, you are likely in **"Threat Detection"** mode. Before making any move, pass it through the **No-Heroics Rule**:

**The "No-Heroics" Practical Test:**

*Does my current plan or new opportunity require me to be "exceptional" (be always at my best version) to survive?*

*Is there a significant risk that it might stop working if I have a bad week (health issues, "life" issues)?*

*Will there be substantial consequences if I pause this?*

*Am I choosing this because I'm scared of inaction?*

**IF YES TO EITHER ONE** of the above questions: **DEFER IT.** It is a gamble disguised as hope. Don't be a hero. Pause, hold your ground and defer until a better option becomes available.

**IF NO TO ALL questions:** Proceed to **Phase 2.**

**PHASE 2: INCOME SORTING** (The 3 Buckets Model)

Stop equating "money coming in" with forward movement. Relief is not stability. Sort your current and potential income to filter them to either of these buckets, in order of priority.

***BUCKET 1: SURVIVAL*** *(The Foundation)*

**Goal:** Cover food, housing, and minimum debt.
**Requirement:** Must be boring and predictable. It cannot depend on high performance or daily motivation. Prioritize and protect this bucket above all.

***BUCKET 2: RECOVERY*** *(The Engine)*

**Goal:** Reduce debt and build "runway".

**Requirement:** Can be irregular or project-based, but must be contained (one-and-done). Must build on top of or parallel to Bucket 1, not replace it.

***BUCKET 3: OPTIONAL UPSIDE*** *(The Future)*

**Goal:** Long-term growth and new experiments.

**Requirement:** Keep this capped and small and only after Buckets 1 and 2 are solid and working.

**Rule:** *Never fund Bucket 1 with Bucket 3 ideas.*

**PHASE 3: DRAIN REMOVAL** (Hustle vs. Recovery Assets)

Side hustles often fail because they add *"context switching"* taxes to an already overloaded system. In the event that a previous action or decision caused some "hustles" to slip through, filter them out at this stage.

Is your extra work a **"Hustle" or a "Recovery Asset"?** What's the difference?

**Hustle:** Extracts energy now for relief now. Depends on your constant presence. If you stop, it breaks.

**Recovery Asset:** Works for you while you recover capacity. It survives low-energy weeks and compounds over time. One-and-done investments of time, effort or money. This is a self-sustaining project that has minimal to zero upkeep.

**Quick Test:** Does this keep working if I step away for two weeks?

**PHASE 4: SURVIVABLE RISK** (The Asymmetric Test)

If you are waiting for certainty, you will wait indefinitely. Instead, look for ***sensible*** or ***good enough*** moves at the moment that produce the most realistic upside and the least downside.

***Before deciding, ask yourself:***

- What is the worst realistic downside?
- Can I absorb that downside (cognitively and financially)?
- Is this decision reversible?

**DECISION RULE:** If the downside is uncapped or in-absorbable, it is **unsafe**. Defer until it becomes safer.

# CHAPTER 1

## WHEN THE NUMBERS WON'T LET YOU BREATHE

There is a specific kind of anxiety that comes from debt that doesn't feel like ordinary stress.

It's not just worry.

It's the sense that every decision carries consequences you can't absorb anymore.

You wake up already tired — not physically, but cognitively. Before the day even starts, your mind is doing math in the background: bills, deadlines, interest, runway, what happens if this doesn't work, what happens if it does but not fast enough.

This kind of pressure quietly degrades decision-making.

. . .

Not because you're weak but because your nervous system is overloaded.

When money is tight, the brain doesn't prioritize creativity or strategy. It prioritizes threat detection. Everything starts to look urgent. Everything feels like it might be the last chance. And that's when people make their most expensive mistakes.

Not dramatic ones.

Small, reasonable ones that stack.

Taking on work that drains you because it pays now.

Chasing ideas that sound promising because standing still feels unbearable.

Overcommitting, underestimating recovery time, ignoring warning signs — not out of recklessness, but out of fear.

Debt anxiety doesn't make you irrational.

It makes you short-term oriented.

. . .

And short-term thinking is dangerous when you're rebuilding.

The paradox is this: the moment you feel the most pressure to act is usually the moment you should slow your decision cycle down, not speed it up.

Most advice fails here because it tells you to "be confident" or "take bold action." Boldness is a luxury when you have no margin. What you need first is **decision safety** — a way to move forward without increasing the risk of collapse.

This book is not about optimism.

It's about reducing errors.

Because when you're under debt, avoiding the wrong moves is often more powerful than chasing the right one.

## The Hidden Cost of Panic Decisions

Panic disguises itself as urgency.

You'll recognize it by the thoughts it produces:

- "I can't afford to wait."
- "I'll figure it out later."

- "This might be my only shot."
- "At least I'll be doing something."

Doing something feels better than doing nothing — even if that something quietly worsens your position.

The real danger isn't one bad decision.

It's a pattern of slightly bad decisions made quickly, without recovery time in between.

Debt doesn't punish you for being slow.

It punishes you for being careless.

That's why the first goal of rebuilding is not growth.

It's stability of judgment.

Before income strategies, before tools, before plans — you need rules that protect you from yourself on bad days.

## Framework: The No-Heroics Rule

You do not take actions that require you to be exceptional in order to survive.

**No heroics means:**

- No plans that only work if you have perfect focus
- No strategies that depend on sustained motivation
- No income streams that collapse if you miss a week
- No bets that assume you'll "figure it out later"

If a plan requires you to be constantly confident, emotionally regulated, productive every day, or socially available on demand, it's not a plan. It's a gamble disguised as hope.

**Practical test**

Before committing to any new opportunity, ask:

- Does this still work if I have a bad week?
- Does this require emotional performance for others?

- Does this increase my future obligations?
- Can I pause this without consequences?
- Am I choosing this because it's good — or because I'm scared?

If it fails two or more checks, defer it.

Deferral is not failure.

It's containment.

## A Reframe That Actually Helps

You are not trying to win right now. You are trying to:

- Stop the bleeding
- Reduce volatility
- Preserve cognitive bandwidth
- Create a floor you can stand on

This is not a motivational phase.

. . .

It's more of an engineering phase.

Progress during this phase looks boring.

That's a feature, not a flaw.

## Small, Safe Action

Write down three decisions you're avoiding.

For each, answer:

- Worst realistic downside
- Best realistic upside
- What changes if you wait 30 days

You're not deciding yet. You're restoring perspective. Clarity returns faster than motivation.

# CHAPTER 2

## INCOME IS NOT THE SAME AS STABILITY

One of the most confusing parts of rebuilding under debt is that you can be working constantly and still feel like you're failing.

Money comes in, but it doesn't stay.

You pay something off, and another obligation appears.

You have a "good" month, followed by two fragile ones.

From the outside, it can look like progress.

From the inside, it feels like you're treading water.

. . .

This creates a subtle but dangerous mental trap: you start equating **income events** with **forward movement**.

A payout feels like relief.

A new client feels like momentum.

A spike feels like hope.

But relief is not stability.

Stability is not about how much money passes through your hands in a moment.

It's about how predictable your next few months are.

Under debt, this distinction gets blurred because time feels compressed. Everything feels urgent. The brain starts overweighting *now* and underweighting *continuity*. That's how people end up chasing income that looks impressive but quietly increases volatility.

What you actually need first is not "more money."

. . .

You need **less fragility**.

## Why Irregular Income Feels Worse Than Low Income

Irregular income is emotionally exhausting because it never lets your nervous system rest.

When income is unpredictable:

- You can't plan beyond the next bill
- You can't recover from setbacks
- You can't say no safely
- Every quiet period feels like danger

This is why someone earning less on a stable salary can feel calmer than someone earning more through irregular gigs. It's not about ambition or grit. It's about **cognitive load**.

The human brain needs some sense of continuity to function well. When income is erratic, your mind stays in a low-grade threat response. Even on good days, part of you is bracing for the next drop.

That constant vigilance drains energy that could otherwise go toward thoughtful decision-making.

. . .

When rebuilding, the right question is not:

"How much can this make?"

It's: "How much uncertainty does this add to my life?"

Income that increases uncertainty may still be income — but it comes at a cost. And under debt, that cost compounds fast.

## The Hidden Cost of "Impressive" Income

Some income looks good on paper but is destabilizing in practice.

Examples:

- Projects that pay well but require intense bursts of energy
- Clients who pay quickly but demand constant availability
- Opportunities that spike income but disappear without warning

These forms of income feel like progress because they move numbers. But they also:

- Increase emotional volatility
- Fragment attention
- Reduce recovery time
- Make planning harder, not easier

When your system is already under strain, volatility becomes dangerous. What you want is not excitement. You want **reliability**.

This doesn't mean you avoid all irregular income. It means you **place it correctly** in your financial structure.

## FRAMEWORK: THE 3 BUCKETS MODEL

This model exists to stop you from accidentally destabilizing yourself while trying to improve.

Think of your income as flowing into three separate buckets. Each bucket has a different job, and confusing them is one of the fastest ways to burn out.

### Bucket 1: Survival Income

This bucket covers:

- Food
- Housing

- Utilities
- Minimum debt payments
- Basic functioning

Survival income must be:

- Predictable
- Boring
- Unglamorous

It should **not** depend on:

- Daily motivation
- Emotional availability
- Constant outreach
- High performance every week

If an income stream cannot reliably support your survival bucket, it is not allowed to replace it.

This is not pessimism.

. . .

It's containment.

## Bucket 2: Recovery Income

This is income that:

- Directly reduces debt
- Builds runway
- Improves future flexibility

Recovery income can be:

- Irregular
- Project-based
- Bursty

But it must be **contained**.

You do the work.
You finish the work.
It pays.
And then it stops demanding attention.

. . .

Contained income is powerful because it creates progress without ongoing strain. It gives you wins that don't require constant maintenance.

### Bucket 3: Optional Upside

This bucket includes:

- Experiments
- New platforms / channels or streams of income
- Speculative ideas
- Long-term growth bets

Bucket 3 is where people put things like:

- New social platforms (YouTube and new/emerging social media, AI etc.)
- Unproven business ideas
- "This might work someday" projects

Under debt, this bucket is **capped**.

. . .

You do not fund your survival with optional upside.

You do not rely on hope to pay bills.

Bucket 3 exists, but it stays small until Buckets 1 and 2 are stable.

## The Rule Most People Violate

They try to fund Bucket 1 with Bucket 3 ideas.

They tell themselves:

- "Once this takes off, everything will be fine."
- "I just need one good break."
- "This is risky, but I don't have a choice."

This is how people end up exhausted, anxious, and stuck in cycles of rebuilding that never quite finish.

This guide exists to help you **sequence correctly**.

First stability.

. . .

Then recovery.

Only then expansion.

## A Practical Reframe

Progress under debt doesn't look like acceleration.
It looks like:

- Fewer emergencies
- More predictable weeks
- Decisions that don't spike anxiety
- Income that doesn't demand constant vigilance

Stability is not boring because you've failed.

It's boring because it's doing its job.

Once stability exists, better opportunities become visible. Not because you're luckier, but because your mind finally has the space to see them.

## Small, Safe Action

Take a sheet of paper and list your current income sources.

For each one, ask:

- Which bucket does this belong in?
- Does it actually belong there, or am I forcing it?
- What happens to my stress level if this disappears for one month?

You're not cutting anything yet.
You're just sorting.
Clarity often arrives before solutions.

## Closing Thought

Rebuilding is not about squeezing more effort out of yourself.

It's about **structuring your income so it stops working against you**.

Once income stops destabilizing your life, it can finally start supporting it.

# CHAPTER 3

## WHY MOST SIDE HUSTLES FAIL UNDER DEBT

Side hustles fail under debt not because they are bad ideas, but because they are added to an already overloaded system.

On paper, a side hustle looks harmless.

It's "extra."

Optional.

A way to improve things.

In reality, under debt, there is no such thing as extra capacity.

. . .

Your time is already constrained.

Your energy is already fragmented.

Your attention is already under pressure.

Adding a side hustle doesn't just add work.

It **changes the shape of your life**.

## The Invisible Problem: Context Switching

The real cost of most side hustles is not effort.

It's **context switching**.

Every time you shift between:

- income streams
- platforms
- roles
- expectations

you pay a cognitive tax.

That tax shows up as:

- slower thinking
- shallow focus
- emotional fatigue
- decision avoidance

Under normal circumstances, this tax is annoying but manageable.

Under debt, it becomes dangerous.

Debt reduces your margin for inefficiency.

What might be survivable in a stable phase becomes destabilizing when you're already stretched.

This is why people feel busy all the time but make no real progress. The system itself is bleeding energy faster than it can recover.

## Why "Doing More" Feels Logical — and Backfires

When money is tight, doing more feels like the responsible response.

You tell yourself:

- "I can handle one more thing."
- "This is temporary."
- "Once this starts paying, I'll drop the others."

The problem is that **temporary load has a habit of becoming permanent**.

Most side hustles don't fail immediately.

They linger.

They require:

- updates
- responses

- maintenance
- emotional availability

Even when they're not actively producing income, they continue consuming attention. And attention, under debt, is your most limited resource.

This is how people end up exhausted without being stable.

## The Side Hustle Illusion

Side hustles often feel safer than committing to one path because they spread risk.

In reality, they often **multiply risk**.

Each additional hustle:

- increases cognitive load
- reduces recovery time
- adds hidden obligations
- fragments momentum

Instead of one system slowly stabilizing, you end up with several fragile systems competing for survival.

The irony is that people under debt often need *fewer* income streams, not more — but structured correctly.

## Why Side Hustles Break the 3 Buckets Model

From Chapter 2, you saw how income must be sequenced into buckets.

Side hustles often fail because they blur those boundaries.

Common mistakes:

- Using speculative ideas to fund survival needs
- Treating optional upside as recovery income
- Expecting unstable projects to provide stability

This forces every income stream to carry too much responsibility.

When one falters, everything shakes.

### Checklist: The "Should I Do This?" Filter

Before starting anything new, run it through this filter — honestly.

Ask yourself:

- **Does this have a clear end?**
- Or does it quietly demand indefinite upkeep?
- **Does it pay without ongoing maintenance?**
- Or does income depend on constant presence?
- **Does it reduce pressure, or add another obligation?**

Relief matters more than potential.

- **Can I stop without consequences?**

If stopping causes damage, it's fragile.

- **Does this align with how I actually function right now?**

Not how you *wish* you functioned on better days.

If the answer reveals fragility, defer it.

. . .

You're not rejecting opportunity.

You're protecting stability.

## The Difference Between "Side Hustle" and "Recovery Asset"

Most people think the solution to debt is more hustle.

The solution is usually **fewer, better-structured efforts**.

### What a Recovery Asset Is

A **recovery asset** is an asset you build **during a constrained period** that:

- reduces future pressure rather than increasing it
- continues to create value without constant input
- does not rely on your emotional availability
- survives low-energy weeks without collapsing
- improves your optionality over time

In plain terms:

A recovery asset works *for* you while you recover capacity.

This is what separates it from hustle.

Hustle extracts energy now in exchange for relief now.

A recovery asset accepts slower returns in exchange for **stability later**.

The goal isn't maximum income.

The goal is **lower fragility**.

## WHAT A RECOVERY ASSET IS NOT

This distinction matters.

A recovery asset is **not**:

- something that pays only while you're actively present
- something that depends on daily motivation
- something that collapses if you miss a week

- something that adds future obligations or maintenance anxiety

If stopping creates damage, it's not a recovery asset.

## CORE CHARACTERISTICS

## (QUICK TEST)

You can identify a recovery asset by asking:

1. **Does this keep working if I step away for two weeks?**
2. **Does it reduce future effort or decisions?**
3. **Does it stabilize income, attention, or credibility over time?**
4. **Does it respect uneven energy?**

If the answer is yes to most of these, you're in recovery-asset territory.

## EXAMPLES OF RECOVERY ASSETS

### 1. A Search-Optimized Evergreen Article (or Small Cluster)

Not frequent blogging.

. . .

Not chasing trends.

One or two **deep, evergreen pieces** that:

- answer a specific recurring question
- are written carefully once
- bring in search traffic quietly over time

Why it's a recovery asset:

- compounds without daily effort
- doesn't require performance
- works while you're offline

This is very different from "content grinding."

## 2. A Recorded Workshop or Talk (Not Live, Not Ongoing)

A single recorded session that:

- solves a specific problem
- can be sold or shared repeatedly

- does not require follow-up calls

Why it's a recovery asset:

- effort is capped
- value is reusable
- no scheduling or emotional labor

The key is **one-and-done**, not an ongoing program.

### 3. A Reusable Tool, Template, or Calculator

For example:

- a pricing calculator
- a planning worksheet
- a decision framework template
- a checklist people return to

Why it's a recovery asset:

- created once

- reduces thinking for others (and you)
- often spreads organically

Tools age better than promises.

### 4. A Back-Catalog of Recorded Content

Not daily posting. A **small, intentional library** of:

- audio reflections
- explanatory videos
- structured lessons

Why it's a recovery asset:

- the work doesn't reset
- older pieces still serve newcomers
- output accumulates instead of disappearing

The catalog matters more than frequency.

### 5. A Permissioned Email List (Even a Small One)

Not aggressive newsletters.

Not constant selling.

A list built slowly where:

- people opt in deliberately
- you can speak without algorithms
- communication is optional, not mandatory

Why it's a recovery asset:

- reduces dependence on platforms
- preserves reach during quiet periods
- gives you a stable channel when needed

Even 300 thoughtful readers beats 10,000 fleeting ones.

## 6. A Clear, Publicly Accessible Point of View

This one is subtle but powerful.

When people know:

- what you think about a problem
- what you won't do
- how you reason under pressure

You spend less time explaining yourself.

Why it's a recovery asset:

- reduces negotiation
- attracts aligned opportunities
- filters out draining ones

Clarity saves energy.

## Why Recovery Assets Matter Under Debt

When you're under financial pressure, **fragility is the enemy**, not slowness.

Recovery assets:

- lower decision fatigue
- smooth income volatility
- create breathing room
- allow you to rest without losing ground

They don't save you overnight.

They make it possible for you to *recover without starting over*.

A recovery asset:

- has a defined scope
- produces reusable output
- does not require constant performance
- creates progress without increasing obligations

- lives in Bucket 2 (Recovery Income)
- has a clear start and end
- pays without demanding presence
- compounds with what you're already creating

It does not fragment your life.

It consolidates it.

## A Hard Truth (and a Helpful One)

If an idea requires you to be:

- consistently energetic
- emotionally available
- visible on demand
- "on" all the time

...it is not compatible with rebuilding under debt.

That doesn't make it a bad idea.

. . .

It makes it a **bad idea for now**.

Timing matters.

## Small, Safe Action

List every active or "almost started" side hustle in your life.

For each one, answer:

- What bucket am I treating this as?
- What bucket does it *actually* belong in?
- What would my stress level look like if I dropped this for 30 days?

You don't need to cut anything today.

You just need to see clearly which things are helping — and which are quietly draining you.

## Closing Thought

Rebuilding under debt is not about proving how much you can endure.

It's about **removing the forces that keep pulling you back into instability**.

When you stop scattering your effort, stability doesn't arrive all at once.

It arrives quietly — and then it sticks.

## Why this chapter matters

Chapter 2 showed you **what stability actually is**.

Chapter 3 shows you **why most attempts to reach it accidentally fail**.

Once you see that pattern, it's hard to unsee it — and that's exactly the point.

# CHAPTER 4

## CHOOSING WHEN EVERYTHING FEELS RISKY

When you're rebuilding under debt, every option feels dangerous.

Doing nothing feels dangerous.

Doing something feels dangerous.

Even good ideas feel risky, because the cost of being wrong feels existential.

This is the point where many people freeze — or swing between paralysis and impulsivity, sometimes in the same week.

. . .

From the outside, it can look like indecision.

From the inside, it feels like self-preservation.

And in many ways, it is.

## Why Everything Feels Risky Under Debt

Debt collapses your margin for error.

When you have savings, time, or support, mistakes are uncomfortable but recoverable. When you're under debt, mistakes feel permanent. Your nervous system responds accordingly.

This is why advice that says "just take action" often backfires. Action without safety doesn't resolve fear — it amplifies it.

The goal in this phase is not confidence.

The goal is **containment**.

You're not trying to eliminate risk.

. . .

You're trying to **choose risks you can survive**.

## The Trap of Waiting for Certainty

Many people delay decisions because they're waiting to feel sure.

They tell themselves:

- "Once I'm more confident, I'll decide."
- "I just need more information."
- "I'll know when it feels right."

Under debt, that moment rarely comes.

Why? Because certainty requires margin — and debt removes margin.

If you wait for certainty, you'll wait indefinitely. And while waiting can be wise, *indefinite waiting* quietly becomes another form of paralysis.

The alternative is not recklessness.

. . .

It's **structured decision-making**.

## Reframing the Goal of a Decision

Most people think decisions are about choosing the *best* option.

Under debt, decisions are about choosing the **least dangerous forward move**.

That's a different skill.

You're not optimizing upside.

You're managing the downside.

Once downside is contained, upside has room to emerge naturally.

## Framework: The Asymmetric Risk Test

This framework exists to help you move forward **without needing certainty**.

For any decision you're considering, ask four questions:

1. **What is the worst realistic downside?**

Not the catastrophic fantasy — the plausible damage.

**2. Can I absorb that downside?**
Financially, emotionally, cognitively.

**3. What is the realistic upside?**
Not the best-case dream — the likely benefit.

**4. Is this decision reversible?**
Can I undo or exit it without lasting harm?

## How to Interpret the Results

You're looking for decisions where:

- Downside is capped
- Loss is survivable
- Upside compounds over time
- Reversibility is high

These decisions don't require bravery.

They require **clarity**.

- Effort is capped
- Output is reusable
- No dependency on others
- No reputational damage if growth is slow
- No ongoing obligation if you pause

It is not guaranteed to succeed.

But it is safe enough to attempt.

That distinction matters.

## The Difference Between "Risky" and "Unsafe"

Many things feel risky under debt.

Not all of them are unsafe.

Risk is unavoidable.

Unsafety is optional.

. . .

An unsafe decision:

- Increases obligations immediately
- Requires constant performance
- Collapses if you miss a week
- Depends on emotional availability

A risky but safe decision:

- Has limited exposure
- Can be paused
- Doesn't punish inconsistency
- Improves clarity even if it fails

Your job is not to avoid risk but to avoid **fragile structures**.

## Why Small Decisions Matter More Than Big Ones

Under stress, people over-focus on big decisions:

- career pivots

- platform choices
- major commitments

In reality, most damage comes from **small, repeated decisions** made without guardrails.

Things like:

- saying yes when you should pause
- adding one more obligation
- delaying recovery time
- ignoring early discomfort

The **Asymmetric Risk Test** works best when applied to *small decisions*. That's where it prevents the most damage.

### A Practical Way to Decide on Bad Days

On days when thinking feels heavy, simplify the test:

Ask only this:

. . .

**"If this goes slightly wrong, does my life get meaningfully harder?"**

If the answer is yes, defer.

Deferral is not avoidance.

It's a strategic pause.

You are allowed to wait until a decision becomes safer.

## Small, Safe Action

Choose one decision you've been stuck on.

Write down:

- Worst realistic downside
- Whether you can absorb it
- Whether it's reversible

You don't need to choose today.

. . .

You just need to **remove the blur**.

Clear thinking often returns once the threat feels bounded.

## Closing Thought

Rebuilding under debt is not about boldness.

It's about **protecting your future self from preventable damage**.

Once you stop demanding certainty from yourself, you regain the ability to move.

Carefully.

Quietly.

And with far fewer regrets.

### Let's assess where you are now:

- Chapter 1 stabilized your thinking
- Chapter 2 redefined progress
- Chapter 3 removed hidden drains

- **Chapter 4 gives you a way to choose safely anyway**

From here on, the work shifts from cognition to **leverage and systems** — where momentum quietly starts to build.

# CHAPTER 5

## EFFORT VS LEVERAGE

Hard work feels virtuous.

Under debt, it can feel like the *only* morally acceptable response.

If things are difficult, you push. If progress is slow, you push harder. Rest starts to feel suspicious. Ease feels undeserved.

The problem is that effort, by itself, does not change outcomes.

It only increases output **in the moment**.

Leverage is what changes outcomes over time.

. . .

Understanding the difference between the two is one of the most important shifts you can make while rebuilding — because exhaustion is not a prerequisite for progress.

## Why Effort Feels Safer Than Leverage

Effort feels controllable.

You can:

- work longer
- say yes more often
- respond faster
- stay busy

All of that gives you the *feeling* of agency.

Leverage, on the other hand, can feel abstract. It requires patience. It doesn't always produce immediate relief. And under debt, immediate relief is seductive.

So people default to effort-heavy strategies:

- live calls

- hourly work
- constant outreach
- always-on availability

These approaches work — temporarily.

But they come with a hidden cost.

They reset to zero every day.

### The Effort Trap

Effort-based progress has a ceiling.

When progress depends on:

- your presence
- your energy
- your emotional availability
- your consistency

then every interruption becomes a threat.

A bad week wipes out momentum.

A low-energy month erases gains.

Rest feels expensive.

This is how people end up trapped in cycles of rebuilding that never quite stabilize. They're working constantly, but nothing accumulates.

Under debt, this is especially dangerous because you don't have the reserves to absorb exhaustion.

## What Leverage Actually Means

Leverage is not a buzzword. It's a simple idea:

**Leverage means your work continues to produce value after you stop actively working on it.**

That's it.

. . .

Leverage shows up when:

- one effort serves multiple purposes
- output can be reused
- progress compounds instead of resetting
- systems replace constant decision-making

Leverage doesn't eliminate effort.

It **changes the return profile of effort**.

## Why Leverage Matters More Than Motivation

Motivation is unreliable.

Energy fluctuates. Life interferes.

Leverage is what allows progress **despite** those realities.

This is why rebuilding phases that rely purely on discipline often fail. They assume a level of consistency that real life rarely provides — especially under stress.

Leverage accepts inconsistency and designs around it.

## Common Sources of Leverage (and Non-Leverage)

**High-leverage activities:**

- Writing that can be reused
- Recorded content
- Frameworks and models
- Systems and templates
- Assets that sell while you're offline

**Low-leverage activities:**

- Live calls
- Real-time availability
- One-off favors
- Work that disappears once delivered
- Anything that requires you to be "on" to function

Some low-leverage work is necessary but it should not be the foundation of your rebuilding.

## Why Writing Is a Leverage Tool (When Used Correctly)

Writing becomes leverage when it:

- captures thinking once
- distributes it many times
- works while you rest
- reduces future explanation

A well-written guide can:

- replace dozens of conversations
- answer questions before they're asked
- earn trust silently
- generate income without scheduling

It is not just a product.

It is a **leverage anchor**.

. . .

It consolidates effort instead of scattering it.

## Framework: Energy-to-Return Mapping

To shift from effort to leverage, you need to see where your energy actually goes.

Create three columns:

**Column 1: Draining Effort**

Activities that:

- consume energy
- don't accumulate
- feel heavy afterward

**Column 2: Neutral Effort**

Activities that:

- maintain stability

- neither drain nor compound significantly

**Column 3: Compounding Effort**

Activities that:

- produce reusable output
- reduce future work
- improve clarity over time

Your goal is not to eliminate effort.

It's to **move weight from Column 1 to Column 3**.

Even small shifts matter.

## The Leverage Test

Before committing to any new work, ask:

- Will this still matter in six months?
- Does this reduce future effort?

- Can this be reused, repurposed, or referenced?
- Does this make my system more stable?

If the answer is no across the board, it's probably effort-heavy.

That doesn't mean you never do it.

It means you **limit** it.

## Why Leverage Feels Slow at First (and Why That's Okay)

Leverage often feels slower in the beginning because:

- it doesn't produce instant feedback
- it doesn't create urgency highs
- it requires upfront thinking

This can be uncomfortable when you're under debt.

But leverage is how you stop rebuilding from scratch every month.

. . .

Once leverage is in place, progress feels quieter — but it sticks.

## A Practical Reframe

You are not trying to squeeze more productivity out of yourself.

You are trying to design a system where:

- effort doesn't evaporate
- rest doesn't undo progress
- bad days don't erase good work

That's what leverage provides.

## Small, Safe Action

List the last five things you worked hard on.

For each, ask:

- Did this reduce my future workload?
- Did this create something reusable?
- Did this make my system more stable?

. . .

No judgment. Just observation.

Patterns become obvious quickly when you look at it this way.

## Closing Thought

Effort gets you through the day.

Leverage gets you through the year.

Rebuilding under debt is not about proving how hard you can work.

It's about **making sure your work finally starts working for you**.

## Where This Leads

Chapters 1–4 helped you:

- stabilize thinking
- define real progress
- remove hidden drains
- decide safely under pressure

. . .

**Chapter 5 marks the pivot** — from survival thinking to sustainable momentum.

# CHAPTER 6

## AI AS A MULTIPLIER, NOT A SAVIOR

AI enters most rebuilding conversations in two extremes.

On one end, it's sold as a miracle — something that will automate your problems away, replace effort, and finally fix everything that feels broken.

On the other end, it's treated as a threat — something that will erase human value, make skills obsolete, and punish anyone who doesn't keep up.

Both views are wrong in the same way.

AI is neither a savior nor a villain.

. . .

It is a **multiplier**.

And like any multiplier, it amplifies whatever you feed into it.

AI replaces friction, not judgment.

## Why AI Feels Especially Tempting Under Debt

When you're under pressure, the appeal of AI is obvious.

You're tired.

Your energy is uneven.

Your attention is stretched.

So the idea of something that can:

- write faster
- decide quicker
- reduce thinking
- remove friction

feels like relief.

. . .

The danger is not in using AI.

The danger is in using it **to escape judgment**.

Under debt, outsourced judgment is expensive.

## What AI Is Actually Good At

AI currently excels at:

- summarizing
- outlining
- reorganizing
- editing
- pattern-matching
- accelerating known tasks

In other words, AI is excellent at **reducing friction after you know what you're doing**.

It is not good at:

- deciding what matters
- choosing values
- understanding your emotional bandwidth
- assessing risk in your specific context

AI does not know what you can absorb. **You do.**

## The Real Risk: Decision Displacement

The quiet danger of AI is not that it replaces work.

It's that it **displaces decision-making**.

This happens when:

- you ask AI what to build instead of deciding your constraints
- you follow suggestions without checking risk
- you let speed replace judgment
- you mistake fluency for truth

Under debt, this is particularly risky because bad decisions compound faster than bad drafts.

A mediocre paragraph is fixable.

A misjudged direction is costly.

## The Rule: Human-in-the-Loop

This guide operates under one non-negotiable rule:

**If a decision affects money, reputation, or long-term direction, a human stays in the loop.**

That human is **you**.

AI can assist.
AI can accelerate.
AI can suggest.

AI cannot decide.

## Where AI Fits in a Leverage-Based System

Used correctly, AI supports leverage by:

- compressing effort
- reducing cognitive load

- speeding up iteration
- preserving energy for judgment

This is especially powerful when your energy is uneven.

On good days, AI helps you move faster.

On bad days, it helps you move at all.

### High-Value Uses of AI (That Don't Undermine You)

When used well, AI is not a substitute for judgment.

It is a way to reduce friction in repetitive, cognitively expensive work—the kind that quietly drains capacity over time.

This matters whether you're running a business, managing a team, or holding a job.

The rule remains the same:

AI supports execution, not direction.

## AI in Business Operations (High-Value, Low-Risk Uses)

### 1. Summarizing complex information quickly

Examples:

Turning long supplier emails into clear bullet points
Summarizing contracts, proposals, or policy documents
Extracting key action items from meeting transcripts

**Why this works:**
You retain decision authority
AI reduces reading fatigue
No strategic judgment is outsourced
You decide *what to do.*
AI helps you see *what's there.*

### 2. Drafting First-Pass Communications

Examples:

Internal emails
Customer replies
Policy explanations
FAQ responses

**Why this works:**
You edit before sending
Tone and judgment remain yours
You avoid emotional over-investment in routine communication

. . .

This is especially valuable under stress, when wording feels heavier than it should.

## 3. Creating Checklists and SOPs

Examples:

Step-by-step processes for recurring tasks
Onboarding checklists
Store opening/closing procedures
Monthly reporting routines

**Why this works:**
Once created, they reduce future thinking
They protect against bad-day mistakes
They increase reliability without requiring motivation
Systems age better than memory.

## 4. Scenario Mapping (Not Decision-Making)

Examples:

"What are possible risks if X happens?"
"What are common failure points in this process?"
"What questions should I ask before committing?"

**Why this works:**
AI generates options, not answers
You evaluate relevance and risk
It expands perspective without replacing judgment
Think of AI as a brainstorming partner, not an authority.

## AI for People Holding a Job

### 5. Clarifying Expectations and Priorities

Examples:

- Summarizing job descriptions into core responsibilities
- Turning vague instructions into clear task lists
- Translating feedback into actionable steps

**Why this works:**

Reduces ambiguity
Prevents overwork caused by misinterpretation
Preserves energy for actual performance
Clarity is a form of leverage.

### 6. Preparing for Conversations (Without Performing)

Examples:

- Organizing talking points for meetings
- Drafting neutral responses to difficult messages
- Reframing emotional reactions into professional language

**Why this works:**

You don't outsource values or boundaries
You reduce emotional labor
You enter conversations steadier
AI helps you prepare—not pretend.

## 7. Learning Acceleration (Not Skill Replacement)

Examples:

Explaining unfamiliar concepts in plain language
Creating summaries of new tools or policies
Turning dense material into examples

**Why this works:**
You still do the thinking
AI compresses the learning curve
It saves time without eroding competence
Understanding remains human.

## What Ties All These Together

In every high-value use:

AI reduces friction
AI lowers cognitive load
AI shortens time-to-clarity
But it does not:
choose direction
assess risk tolerance
weigh long-term consequences
decide what matters

That line matters most under pressure.

These uses **do not replace thinking**.

. . .

They reduce friction around thinking and protect it from exhaustion.

That's the sweet spot.

## Low-Value (and Risky) Uses of AI

AI becomes dangerous when used to:

- decide business direction
- assess emotional readiness
- determine financial risk
- replace lived context
- manufacture confidence

> If you find yourself thinking, "I'll just let the tool decide," that's a signal to pause.

AI cannot feel consequences. **You will.**

## A Practical Way to Use AI Without Losing Yourself

Before using AI for any task, decide:

- What am I asking it to help with?

- What am I not outsourcing?

A useful rule of thumb:
Use AI to **speed up execution**, never to **choose direction**.

Execution can be revised.

Direction is expensive to undo.

## Small, Safe Action

Pick one task you've been avoiding because it feels heavy.

Ask:

- Is this a thinking task or a friction task?

If it's friction (formatting, structuring, editing), let AI help.

If it's thinking (deciding what to do next, whether to commit, how much risk to take), keep it human.

This distinction alone removes a lot of overwhelm.

## Closing Thought

AI does not save you.

But it can give you back:

- time
- energy
- clarity
- momentum

when you use it deliberately.

You don't rebuild by replacing yourself.

You rebuild by **protecting your judgment and removing everything that makes using it harder**.

# CHAPTER 7

## SYSTEMS FOR BAD DAYS

Most systems are designed for good days.

Design for bad days, not ideal ones.

They assume:

- steady motivation
- clear thinking
- emotional regulation
- uninterrupted time

And when those conditions aren't met, the system collapses—not because the person failed, but because the design was fragile.

Under debt, this happens constantly.

Bad days are not exceptions.

They are part of the environment.

If your progress only works when you feel okay, it's not a system.

It's a wish.

## Why Bad Days Matter More Than Good Ones

Good days feel productive, but they're not the real test.

On good days, almost anything works.

You have energy. You have optimism. You can push.

Bad days are where progress either: quietly survives or resets to zero.

. . .

This is why people feel like they're always starting over. They build momentum on good days, then lose it the moment life intrudes.

Debt amplifies this problem because bad days come with extra weight:

- financial anxiety
- decision fatigue
- fear of falling behind

Designing for bad days is not pessimistic.

It's realistic.

## The Core Shift: From Motivation to Reliability

Most advice tries to increase motivation.

That's the wrong lever.

Motivation fluctuates.

. . .

Reliability compounds.

A reliable system does not ask:

- "How do I feel today?"
- "Am I inspired?"
- "Do I have momentum?"

It asks:

- "What still works today?"
- "What is the smallest action that keeps the system alive?"

Progress under debt is less about speed and more about **continuity**.

## What Makes a System Fragile

A system breaks easily when it:

- requires long, uninterrupted time blocks
- has no clear stopping points

- depends on emotional readiness
- punishes inconsistency
- treats missed days as failure

Fragile systems turn normal human variation into self-judgment.

That judgment then drains the energy you need to continue.

### What Makes a System Resilient

A resilient system:

- has a minimum viable version
- works in short bursts
- allows pauses without penalty
- has clear boundaries
- treats bad days as expected input

Resilient systems do not demand excellence.

. . .

They demand **presence**.

## Framework: The Low-Energy Production System

This framework exists to keep progress alive when energy is limited.

It has four parts.

### A. MINIMUM VIABLE OUTPUT

Minimum viable output is the **smallest unit of progress that keeps the system alive**—even on days when energy, clarity, or motivation are low.

It is not about quality, ambition, or completeness.

It is about **continuity**.

If your system only counts progress when conditions are ideal, it will fail you the moment life interferes—which is often.

**Minimum viable output** exists so progress can continue **without requiring heroics**.

## Examples Across Real Work Contexts

### 1. For Someone Building a Product or Business

Instead of:
"Finish the product feature"
"Launch the next version"
"Finalize the entire offer"

Minimum viable output might be:

- Write the problem statement for one feature
- Document one assumption the product depends on
- Outline the steps for one operational process
- Fix one known friction point
- Update one internal checklist or SOP

On bad days, **clarity beats completion**.

Capturing one decision or removing one unknown keeps momentum alive.

## 2. For Entrepreneurs Managing Operations

Instead of:

"Clean up operations"
"Optimize the workflow"
"Improve margins"

**Minimum viable output might be:**

- Review yesterday's numbers and note one anomaly
- Update one pricing or cost assumption
- Identify one recurring operational mistake
- Write down one rule to prevent a future error

This protects the system from silent decay—without requiring a full overhaul.

## 3. For Someone in a Corporate Role

Instead of:

"Be productive today"
"Make progress on the project"
"Catch up on everything"

. . .

**Minimum viable output might be:**

- Clarify one ambiguous task
- Send one alignment email
- Prepare talking points for one meeting
- Document one decision or dependency
- Complete one task that reduces future rework

This prevents backlog anxiety from turning into paralysis.

### 4. For Knowledge Workers Under Heavy Cognitive Load

Instead of:
"Think through the whole strategy"
"Solve the entire problem"

Minimum viable output might be:

- Write down what you *don't* know yet
- List the constraints that cannot change
- Identify the next irreversible decision
- Capture one open question for later

Progress does not always look like answers.

Sometimes it looks like **containment**.

### Why This Works (The Principle Beneath It)

Minimum viable output works because it:

- lowers the activation energy to start
- avoids all-or-nothing thinking
- preserves continuity without exhaustion
- keeps systems from resetting to zero

It replaces the question
"Can I do this properly today?" with
**"What keeps this alive today?"**
That shift alone is often enough to keep people from quitting.

## B. USE PREDEFINED TEMPLATES

When energy is low, decisions are more expensive than effort.

Most people assume bad days fail because they lack motivation. In reality, bad days fail because they require too many small choices before any work can even begin.

. . .

Templates exist to remove those choices.

A predefined template is not about rigidity or bureaucracy.

It is about **protecting judgment by eliminating avoidable decisions**.

On bad days, you should not be deciding *how* to do work.

You should only be deciding **whether** to do it.

## What a Template Really Is

A template is any repeatable structure that answers questions in advance, such as:

- What does "done" look like?
- What comes first?
- What can be ignored?
- Where does this stop?

Templates convert open-ended work into **bounded work**.

. . .

That boundary is what makes bad-day progress possible.

## Examples Across Real Work Contexts

### 1. For Entrepreneurs and Business Owners

Instead of approaching work as:
"What should I work on today?"
Templates might include:

- A daily operations checklist
- A weekly review outline (numbers → issues → decisions)
- A pricing or purchasing decision framework
- A standard way to respond to customer issues

On bad days, you don't improvise.

You follow the structure and stop.

This prevents reactive decision-making from quietly damaging the business.

### 2. For Product Builders and Project Leads

Instead of:
"Figure out how to move this forward"

Templates might include:

- A feature scoping template
- A decision memo format
- A project update structure
- A risk checklist before committing

This ensures that even partial progress is **coherent**, not scattered.

The work stays aligned even when your energy doesn't.

### 3. For People in Corporate Roles

Instead of:
"Handle emails / meetings / tasks as they come"

Templates might include:

- A meeting prep template (purpose, decisions, risks)

- A standard format for status updates
- A response framework for difficult emails
- A checklist for recurring reports or reviews

This reduces:

- overthinking
- emotional labor
- rework caused by ambiguity

Clarity replaces vigilance.

### 4. For Managers and Team Leads

Instead of:
"Deal with people issues as they arise"

Templates might include:

- A 1-on-1 conversation structure
- A feedback framework
- A performance review outline

- A conflict documentation format

Templates here don't dehumanize the work.

They **protect fairness and consistency** when emotions are high.

### Why Templates Matter Under Pressure

Under debt or sustained stress:

- decision fatigue accumulates quickly
- small mistakes compound
- improvisation becomes risky

Templates:

- lower cognitive load
- prevent drift
- keep work within safe bounds

They turn bad days from liabilities into **manageable inputs**.

### The Quiet Power of Templates

Templates do not make you mechanical.

They make you:

- steadier
- less reactive
- less vulnerable to mood and stress

They ensure that your worst days still move things forward—without asking you to be exceptional. Templates don't replace thinking—they preserve it for the decisions that actually matter.

## C. BUILD IN STOP POINTS

Most work expands to fill whatever space you give it.
On good days, that feels productive.
On bad days, it becomes punishing.

Stop points exist to protect you from **open-ended effort**—the kind that never feels finished and quietly drains more than it gives.

. . .

A stop point is a **predefined boundary** that tells you when to stop working, regardless of whether the work feels complete.

This is not about lowering standards.

It is about **preventing exhaustion from masquerading as commitment**.

## What a Stop Point Really Is

A stop point answers one simple question in advance:

*When does this task end for today?*

Without that answer, work has no edges—and edge-less work is dangerous under pressure.

Stop points turn effort into **contained effort**.

## Examples Across Real Work Contexts

### 1. For Entrepreneurs and Business Owners

Instead of:

"Work on the business until it's better"

Stop points might look like:

- Review metrics for 30 minutes, then stop

- Address only the top three issues surfaced today
- Make one pricing or purchasing decision, then pause
- Improve one process, not the entire system

This prevents over-intervention, which often causes more damage than inaction.

## 2. For Product Builders and Project Leads

Instead of:
"Keep refining until it's right"

Stop points might include:

- One review pass, no revisions beyond that
- Clarify scope, risks, and next steps—nothing more
- Document decisions made today and stop

This keeps progress moving without perfectionism stalling it.

### 3. For People in Corporate Roles

Instead of:
"Stay until everything is handled"

Stop points might be:

- Clear the inbox to zero decisions, not zero emails
- Prepare talking points for tomorrow's meeting, then stop
- Complete one task that reduces future rework

This protects against the quiet burnout caused by invisible, endless labor.

### 4. For Managers and Team Leads

Instead of:
"Keep thinking about how to fix the team"

Stop points might include:

- Document one observation per person
- Prepare one conversation, not all of them
- Decide one action to take next week

. . .

This keeps leadership work thoughtful, not reactive.

## Why Stop Points Matter More on Bad Days

On bad days:

- energy is finite
- focus degrades quickly
- emotional labor is heavier

Without stop points, you don't just work—you **leak**.

Stop points allow you to:

- exit before resentment builds
- preserve capacity for tomorrow
- return to work without dread

They make sustainability possible.

### Stop Points vs. Quitting

Stopping is not quitting.
Quitting abandons the system.
Stopping preserves it.

This distinction matters because people often push past reasonable limits out of fear—fear of falling behind, of appearing uncommitted, of losing ground.

Stop points remove that fear by making stopping **part of the system**, not a failure of will.

Work that never ends will eventually end you. Stop points prevent that.

## D. SEPARATE CREATION FROM COMPLETION

One of the fastest ways to exhaust yourself is to create and perfect at the same time.

Creation is generative.

Completion is evaluative.

. . .

They require different energy, different attention, and different emotional states. When you force them to coexist, progress slows and frustration rises.

It shows up when:

- you try to design a process and optimize it simultaneously
- you draft a proposal while second-guessing its reception
- you start solving a problem while already worrying about whether the solution will be approved
- you outline a plan while mentally running through everything that could go wrong

On bad days, this overlap becomes especially costly.

Separating creation from completion allows work to move forward without demanding perfection in the moment. You generate first, evaluate later—when energy and perspective are better.

This is not about lowering standards.

. . .

It's about **sequencing effort so standards don't paralyze progress**.

Resilient systems separate:

- drafting from editing
- thinking from polishing
- output from evaluation

On bad days, you create without judgment.
On better days, you refine.
This keeps momentum intact.

## Why Consistency Is a Misleading Goal

Consistency is often framed as daily output.
That's misleading

True consistency is **not breaking the chain of intention**, even when output is small.

Missing days doesn't break consistency.
Abandoning the system does.

A system that tolerates missed days is more consistent than one that collapses after them.

## Designing Progress That Forgives You

Under debt, shame is corrosive.
Missed days become evidence:

- that you're failing
- that you're unreliable
- that this won't work

A resilient system does not keep score that way.

It assumes:

- fluctuations
- interruptions
- emotional weather

And it continues anyway.

## A Practical Example

Instead of saying:
"I need to make meaningful progress today."
Which quietly implies:

- long hours
- sustained focus
- emotional readiness
- visible results

A forgiving system reframes the goal as:
"What is one action today that keeps this from getting worse?"

**For an entrepreneur, that might mean:**

- reviewing one key number and noting an anomaly
- documenting one decision instead of solving everything
- fixing one recurring friction point
- postponing a risky move rather than forcing progress

. . .

**For someone rebuilding personally, it might mean:**

- paying attention to one obligation instead of the entire picture
- clarifying one next step instead of planning the whole future
- choosing rest intentionally rather than collapsing into avoidance

Some days, this will feel almost disappointingly small.

But the system doesn't collapse.

And that's the point.

Progress that forgives you does not ask whether you showed up at your best.

It asks whether the situation is **slightly more stable** than it was yesterday.

## Small, Safe Action

Design your minimum viable output for this project.

Write it down.
Make it so small it feels almost silly — but still meaningful.

Then ask:

- Can I do this on my worst day?
- Would doing this keep the project alive?

If yes, your system will survive.

## Closing Thought

You do not fail because you're inconsistent.

You fail when your systems demand a version of you that doesn't exist every day.

Progress under debt does not come from pushing harder.

It comes from **designing work that forgives you and keeps going anyway**.

# CHAPTER 8

## WHY CONSISTENCY FEELS HARDER THE SECOND TIME

One of the most confusing experiences in rebuilding is realizing that consistency feels harder now than it did the first time.

You know what to do.

You've done hard things before.

You're not starting from ignorance.

And yet, effort feels heavier. Momentum feels fragile. Even small commitments carry weight.

This can be deeply unsettling.

. . .

Many people interpret this as a personal decline — as evidence that they've lost discipline, confidence, or capacity.

That interpretation is wrong.

What you're experiencing is not weakness.

It's **memory**. Resistance is often self-protection.

## The Cost of Experience

The first time you build something, you're protected by a kind of innocence.

You don't know:

- how long things can take
- how easily momentum can disappear
- how painful reversals feel
- how exhausting false starts can be

That ignorance can look like confidence.

. . .

The second time, you don't have that protection.
You remember:

- the effort it required
- the stress it created
- the uncertainty that never fully went away
- the moment things unraveled

Your nervous system doesn't forget these things, even if your conscious mind wants to move on.

This makes consistency feel heavier — not because you're less capable, but because now you're **more informed**.

## Why Motivation Doesn't Work the Same Way Anymore

Motivation thrives on novelty.

The first time, novelty is everywhere:

- new goals
- new identity

- new momentum
- new hope

The second time, novelty is gone.

You're not imagining the difficulty. You are trying to draw energy from a source that has already been depleted.

This is why advice that focuses on "finding your why" often fails rebuilders. You already know your why. Knowing it doesn't make the work lighter.

Consistency the second time around does not come from excitement.

It comes from **safety**.

## The Protective Nature of Resistance

Resistance is often framed as self-sabotage.

In rebuilding phases, it is usually self-protection.

Your mind is asking:

- Is this worth the cost?
- Will this drain me again?
- What happens if this fails too?

These are not lazy questions.

They are **boundary-setting questions**.

The problem isn't that these questions exist.

The problem is ignoring them.

When you push past resistance without answering it, your system pushes back harder later.

## The Grief No One Talks About

There is a quiet grief that accompanies rebuilding.

You are not just trying again.

You are grieving:

- lost time
- lost confidence
- lost simplicity
- the version of yourself who didn't know how hard this could be

Grief consumes energy.

Unacknowledged grief consumes even more.

This is why rebuilding often feels emotionally heavier than starting fresh. You're carrying the weight of comparison — not to others, but to your past self.

## Why "Just Be Disciplined" Is the Wrong Instruction

Discipline assumes a neutral emotional baseline.

Rebuilders do not have that luxury.

You are operating with:

- heightened risk awareness

- reduced margin for error
- emotional residue from previous outcomes

Demanding the same output under different conditions is not discipline.

It's denial.

Consistency the second time requires **redesign**, not resolve.

## What Sustainable Consistency Actually Looks Like Now

Consistency after failure is quieter.

It looks like:

- shorter sessions
- fewer commitments
- slower visible progress
- less emotional intensity
- more internal negotiation

. . .

This is not regression.

It is **adaptation**. This is necessary for rebuilding.

A system that respects your history will outperform one that ignores it.

## Reframing the Goal of Consistency

The goal is no longer "show up every day."

The goal is:
"Do not re-traumatize myself in the process of rebuilding."

Consistency that requires emotional suppression is not sustainable.

Consistency that allows caution, pacing, and consent is.

## A Practical Shift That Changes Everything

Instead of asking:

> "Why can't I be consistent anymore?"

. . .

Ask:

"What would consistency look like if it didn't require self-betrayal?"

This question opens design space.

It allows:

- smaller promises
- gentler timelines
- clearer boundaries
- systems that feel safe enough to return to

Consistency is not about force.
It's about **trust**.

## Small, Safe Action

Write down one expectation you have of yourself that belonged to your *first* build.

Then ask:

- Is this still fair?

- Does this reflect my current reality?
- What would a kinder version look like?

You are allowed to update your standards.

## Closing Thought

Consistency doesn't feel harder because you're worse at this.

It feels harder because you know what's at stake.

That awareness is not a flaw.

It's the reason your next rebuild has a chance to last.

# CHAPTER 9

## PROGRESS WITHOUT ANNOUNCEMENTS

Let's talk about the subtle pressure that appears once you decide to rebuild.

It's not external at first. It sounds internal.

A quiet urge to:

- explain what you're doing
- justify your choices
- signal momentum
- reassure others (and yourself) that this time is different

This urge feels harmless. Even healthy.

In reality, under debt, it's often one of the fastest ways to drain energy and destabilize progress.

## Why We Feel the Need to Announce

Announcements serve a psychological function.

They:

- create a sense of commitment
- invite encouragement
- reduce the loneliness of starting again
- signal identity ("I'm doing something")

For first-time builders, this can be motivating.

For rebuilders, it often backfires.

Because announcements create **pressure before stability exists.**

## The Cost of Visibility Under Debt

Visibility adds weight.

Once you announce something, you don't just have the work — you also have:

- expectations
- imagined judgment
- comparison
- the need to maintain a narrative

Even supportive reactions create subtle obligations:

- to update
- to explain delays
- to perform confidence

Under debt, this extra layer matters because you are already operating with:

- limited margin

- fragile energy
- heightened self-monitoring

Adding social pressure increases volatility.

## Why Quiet Progress Is Safer

Quiet progress removes an entire category of risk.

When you work privately:

- timelines can stretch without shame
- direction can change without explanation
- bad weeks don't feel like public failure
- success doesn't need immediate validation

**Privacy protects experimentation.**

And rebuilding is, at its core, an experiment.

## Public Accountability vs Private Reliability

Public accountability is often framed as necessary for follow-through but that's not universally true.

. . .

There are two types of accountability:

- **external accountability** (people watching)
- **structural accountability** (systems that continue)

Under debt, structural accountability is far more reliable.
Systems don't judge.
Systems don't compare.
Systems don't rush you.
They simply wait for you to return.

## The Illusion of Motivation Through Exposure

Exposure can feel motivating because it creates urgency.

Urgency, however, is not the same as stability.

Urgency spikes output in the short term.

Stability preserves output over time.

Most people rebuilding don't fail because they lack urgency.

They fail because urgency exhausts them before systems can form.

## Why Comparison Is Especially Toxic During Rebuilding

Comparison is unavoidable once progress is public. Even if you don't seek it out, it finds you.

You start measuring:

- pace
- milestones
- confidence
- visibility

Against people with:

- different timelines
- different resources
- different risks

**This distorts perception.**

. . .

What looks like slow progress in public might be extraordinary progress in private — given your constraints.

## The Framework: The Next Safe Step

At this stage, you are not choosing bold moves.

You are choosing safe **continuation**.

**The Next Safe Step** is:

- not the best step
- not the fastest step
- not the most impressive step

**It is the step that:**

- does not increase obligations
- does not require confidence
- does not demand performance
- does not expose fragile progress

Safe steps compound because they don't scare you away. Quiet rebuilding compounds better.

## Why Privacy Strengthens Consistency

Privacy reduces:

- self-monitoring
- narrative maintenance
- emotional labor

This frees energy for:

- thinking
- building
- adjusting
- continuing

The fewer people watching, the fewer parts of yourself you need to manage.

That matters when energy is limited.

## A Common Fear (and the Truth Behind It)

Many people worry that if they don't announce progress, they'll lose momentum.

In practice, the opposite often happens.

Momentum grows when:

- pressure is low
- permission to move slowly exists
- work feels contained
- success is not immediately scrutinized

Quiet work is easier to return to.

## What "Private" Actually Means

Privacy does not mean secrecy.
It means **selectivity**.

You choose:

- who knows
- when they know
- what they need to know

You are not hiding.

You are pacing.

### Small, Safe Action

Pick one area of your rebuilding that you have felt compelled to explain or justify.

Ask yourself:

- Who is this explanation for?
- What pressure does this create?
- What would happen if I let this progress quietly for 30 days?

Silence is not avoidance. It's often a strategy.

## Closing Thought

Rebuilding under debt is not a performance.

It does not need applause.
It does not need witnesses.
It does not need constant validation.
It needs **space**.
Space to make careful decisions.
Space to build systems that survive bad days.

Space to let progress become real before it becomes visible.

Quiet progress is not weak. It's **protected**.

# CHAPTER 10

## WHAT STABILITY ACTUALLY FEELS LIKE

Stability rarely announces itself.

It does not arrive with fireworks or a sudden sense of triumph. There is no single moment when you realize, definitively, that you are "safe now." That expectation—of clarity, of certainty, of relief all at once—is one of the last myths this guide asks you to let go of.

Stability is quieter than that.

It arrives gradually, almost invisibly, and often only becomes obvious in retrospect—when you notice what is no longer happening.

## What Stability Is Not

Stability is not the absence of effort.
It is not the absence of fear.
It is not the absence of debt.
And it is not constant happiness.

People often imagine stability as a feeling—calm, confidence, ease. But feelings are volatile. They change with sleep, health, stress, and circumstance.

If stability depended on how you felt, it would be fragile.

What you are building instead is something sturdier.

## What Stability Actually Feels Like (From the Inside)

Stability feels like **less noise**.

Less background math running in your head.
Less urgency in ordinary decisions.
Less pressure to react immediately.

You still think about money—but it no longer hijacks your attention. It becomes one input among many, not the dominant signal.

You notice that pauses feel safer. Silence doesn't automatically mean danger. A quiet week does not trigger the same spiral it once did.

You are able to stop working without panic.
That is not laziness.
That is **capacity**.

## The Measurable Signs of Stability

Stability is not just emotional. It leaves a trail.

You can measure it.

Here is what it looks like in the real world:

- You can predict your next 30–60 days with reasonable accuracy
- Missed days do not destroy momentum
- Income does not depend on your constant presence
- You say "no" more often—and regret it less
- You recover faster from setbacks
- Decisions take less time and cost less energy
- Progress no longer resets to zero

## The Shift From Survival to Agency

Earlier in this guide, decisions were about **not making things worse**.

That phase matters. It is not small or shameful.

. . .

But stability marks a transition.

Once your systems can survive bad days, once your effort compounds instead of evaporates, once your judgment is protected instead of outsourced—you regain something essential:

**Agency.**

Not the loud, performative kind.

The quiet kind that shows up as choice.

Choice about where to put your energy.

Choice about which risks are worth taking.

Choice about when to rest.

Agency is the real dividend of rebuilding.

## Why Stability Makes Life Feel Larger

Here is something rarely acknowledged:

When you are under debt-induced instability, your world shrinks.

You think shorter-term.

You avoid complexity.

You make yourself smaller to survive.

Stability reverses this.

As volatility decreases, your thinking horizon expands. You begin to consider not just what is urgent, but what is meaningful.

This is where rebuilding becomes unexpectedly satisfying.

Not because everything is easy—but because your effort finally aligns with your values.

## The Gift to the People Around You

Stability is not a solo achievement.
When your life is less volatile, the people around you feel it.

You become:

- more present
- more patient
- more reliable
- less reactive

You stop borrowing emotional energy from others just to get through the day. You stop carrying urgency into conversations that don't require it.

This is one of the quiet triumphs of rebuilding: the way your steadiness becomes a form of care.

For partners.
For family.
For friends.
For anyone who has been holding their breath with you.

## Why Rebuilding Under Debt Can Be Deeply Fulfilling

This may surprise you, but it's true:
Rebuilding under constraint often produces a more meaningful life than building with ease.

Why?

Because you learn:

- what actually matters
- what drains you versus what sustains you
- how to design instead of force
- how to protect judgment under pressure

You stop mistaking intensity for importance.

You stop equating exhaustion with virtue.

You build with intention.

**That skill does not disappear when the debt does.**

## The Quiet Confidence That Follows

There's a certain confidence that comes from luck.

And there is a confidence that comes from repetition.

Stability produces the second kind.

It is not loud.

It does not need validation.

It does not rush to prove itself.

It shows up as trust—in your systems, in your pacing, in your ability to recover.

That trust is earned.

## A Final Reframe

Rebuilding under debt is often framed as something to endure.

But for many who complete it thoughtfully, it becomes something else entirely:

A recalibration.

A stripping away.

A return to essentials.

You don't just rebuild your finances.

You rebuild your relationship with effort.

With time.

With risk.

With yourself.

And once that is rebuilt, everything else becomes more possible.

## Closing Thought on This Final Chapter

Stability is not a finish line.

It is a foundation.

It allows you to build again—this time without panic, without heroics, without self-betrayal.

If you've made it this far—through uncertainty, restraint, quiet work, and careful design—know this:

You are not merely surviving.

You are becoming someone who knows how to rebuild.

And that knowledge, once earned, does not leave you.

It stays. It compounds. It carries forward—into whatever comes next.

# CLOSING

This book began with a simple premise: when you're rebuilding under debt, clarity matters more than speed, and judgment matters more than intensity.

If there is one idea to carry forward, it is this—progress does not require you to become someone else. It does not demand constant confidence, perfect discipline, or heroic effort. It asks only that you make fewer damaging decisions, protect your energy where it matters most, and design your life so it can keep moving even when conditions aren't ideal.

You may not feel transformed after reading this. That's intentional. What you may notice instead, over time, is a quieter mind, steadier choices, and a growing ability to pause without panic. These are not dramatic wins, but they are the kind that last.

Return to this guide when things feel noisy again. Use it not as a plan to follow, but as a reference point—to remind yourself how to think when pressure is high and margin is thin. Rebuilding is rarely linear, but it is possible. And done carefully, it can leave you not just more stable, but more grounded than you were before.

**Stay in touch**

If this helped, join the newsletter for updates, tools, and new releases.

**join.steadyhandpress.com**

## ON INFLUENCE AND CONTEXT

This book isn't rooted in academic research or formal financial theory, though many of its ideas overlap with them. The frameworks here are informed by behavioral economics, cognitive load theory, trauma-informed thinking, and minimalist systems design—but filtered through lived experience rather than textbooks.

I didn't set out to build a perfect model. I set out to build something that could survive bad days, limited energy, and real constraints. Where established ideas helped clarify what I was experiencing, I leaned on them. Where they didn't, I let reality lead.

If this book has authority, it comes from careful thinking under pressure—not certainty, not credentials, and not pretending there's a single right way out.

## ON THE MAKING OF THIS BOOK

This book was developed independently, shaped over time by lived experience and sustained reflection. It reflects an attempt to think clearly under constraint, and to translate that thinking into forms others might find usable. Any clarity it offers is the result of that process. Any limitations remain my own.

# ABOUT THE AUTHOR

**Cecilia Regina Aquino Blanquera** is a writer and independent publisher based in the Philippines. She writes about decision-making, financial stress, and systems design from lived experience, focusing on how people navigate periods of cognitive overload and constraint without relying on motivational or heroic narratives.

Her work centers on clarity, orientation, and harm reduction—especially in situations where confidence is unreliable and margin is thin.

She is the founder of **Steady Hand Press**, an independent imprint for durable, practitioner-led nonfiction.

***Rebuilding Under Debt: Thinking Clearly When Everything Is a Blur*** is her first book-length work.

*Rebuilding Under Debt: Thinking Clearly When Everything Is a Blur* is a practical guide for people who can't afford another wrong move.

When you're under debt, the hardest part isn't the math.

It's that everything starts to blur.

Decisions feel heavier. Urgency crowds out judgment. Small mistakes carry consequences you don't have room to absorb. In that state, even good advice can make things worse—because it assumes clarity you no longer have.

This is not a motivational book. It doesn't ask you to hustle harder, think positively, or move faster. Instead, it offers a calmer and more reliable approach: restoring judgment before action, so you don't make the situation worse while trying to fix it.

Written for those navigating financial pressure, decision fatigue, and uneven energy, ***Rebuilding Under Debt*** helps readers:

- reduce costly mistakes under pressure
- distinguish income from stability
- avoid side hustles that quietly increase fragility
- make safer decisions without needing certainty
- design progress that survives bad days

Calm, grounded, and deeply practical, this book is not about getting ahead.

It's about staying intact long enough for rebuilding to begin.